Reading Options
for Achievement

TABLE OF CONTENTS

Reading Options for Achievement
Level D

Acknowledgements
Product Development: Kent Publishing Services
Design and Production: Signature Design Group
Illustrations: Kevin Brown, Top Dog Studios
Photos: 7, whales, James Watt, Animals/Animals; 21, Godzilla, Archive Photos; 22, movie making, Archive Photos; 40, space station, NASA; 41, Canada Hand, NASA; 49, children, Design Elements; 51, Anne Frank, Magic Johnson, Archive Photos; 55, Tiger Woods, Archive Photos; 60, boat at Ellis Island, Archive Photos/American Stock; 61, people at Ellis Island, Archive Photos; 62, people at Ellis Island, Archive Photos; 68, Ellis Island building, Archive Photos; 73, Mars Surveyor, NASA; 74, robot, NASA; 75, Mars Rover, NASA; 76, Mars Surveyor logo, NASA; 78, Viking I, NASA; 79, views of Mars, NASA; 84, possum, Brent P. Kent, Animals/Animals; possum, Animals/Animals

ISBN 1-56936-673-X
© 2001 Options Publishing, Inc.
P.O. Box 1749
Merrimack, NH 03054-1749
TOLL FREE: 800-782-7300 • FAX: 866-424-4056

www.optionspublishing.com

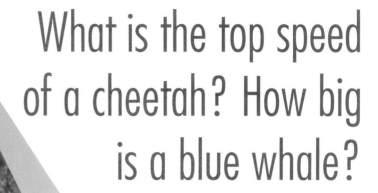

What is the top speed of a cheetah? How big is a blue whale?

Did you notice that you used numbers to answer each question? We use math and numbers in everyday life, especially when we read and learn about the world around us.

In this unit you will learn some interesting facts and details about animals. You will also find comparisons among things as you read. Notice how numbers are used to explain facts and make comparisons.

The elephant is almost as big as the tree.

Think About It

Have you ever said something is "as big as a house"? Think of two things that are big. Write a sentence to compare one to the other.

_____

_____

_____

A Great Mammal

Answer this riddle: What animal lives in water and swims like a fish, but is not a fish? Its newborn baby might gain 200 pounds in one day. This animal can stay under water for more than an hour, but it needs to breathe air! Have you guessed it? It is a whale!

Whales live in water just like fish, but whales are **mammals**. Mammals give birth to live babies. Most fish lay eggs. Mammals feed their babies with milk. Fish do not feed their babies. In some ways, whales are more like dogs or cats than fish. Mammals are warm-blooded. Their body temperature stays about the same no matter how warm or cold it is. Fish are cold-blooded. Their body temperature changes when the temperature of the water changes.

Vocabulary

mam•mal an animal that is warm-blooded, feeds its young with milk, and is usually covered with hair

React • Find Facts and Details

What happens to a whale's temperature when the whale swims into colder water?

_____

_____

Whales can grow to be huge! The blue whale is the biggest. It can grow to over one hundred feet long. Compare that to a person who is six feet tall. A killer whale grows to be about thirty feet long.

A killer whale can swim as fast as a blue whale—about twenty-five miles per hour. This is about the same speed that a car travels along a suburban street.

If a blue whale and a killer whale were to **compete** in a race, who do you think would win? The blue whale would probably win. Its great size would let it keep its speed up longer. How fast do you think you can swim? A strong swimmer can swim one mile in about fifteen minutes.

There are about seventy-five kinds of whales. Scientists divide them into two groups: **baleen** whales and toothed whales. Toothed whales, such as dolphins and porpoises, have teeth. Baleen whales, such as the blue whale, do not have teeth. They have hundreds of thin plates that hang from their jaws. Baleen is a lot like our fingernails. It collects food as the whale swims through the water.

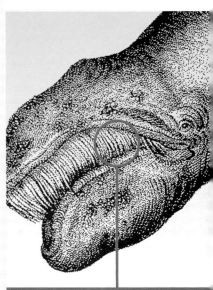

baleen

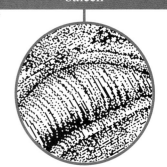

React • Make a Comparison

In the story, three animals are compared in size. Which of the following mammals is about the size of a large bicycle?

Ⓐ a human   Ⓒ a killer whale

Ⓑ a blue whale   Ⓓ a cat

Some kinds of whales travel in groups or herds. There can be as many as 1,000 in a herd of dolphins. They look like an acrobatic troupe, diving and jumping through the water. Other whales, like the blue whale or the **sei** whale, live in family groups.

Many whales **migrate** between cold and warm places. In summer, they live in the Arctic and Antarctic regions. These cold waters have lots of food. During the winter months, the whales migrate to warmer waters.

Focus on Facts and Details

★ **When you read it is important to pay attention to details. You may be asked to recall, or remember, details you have read.**

1. Complete the word web using facts and details about fish and whales from the article "A Great Mammal."

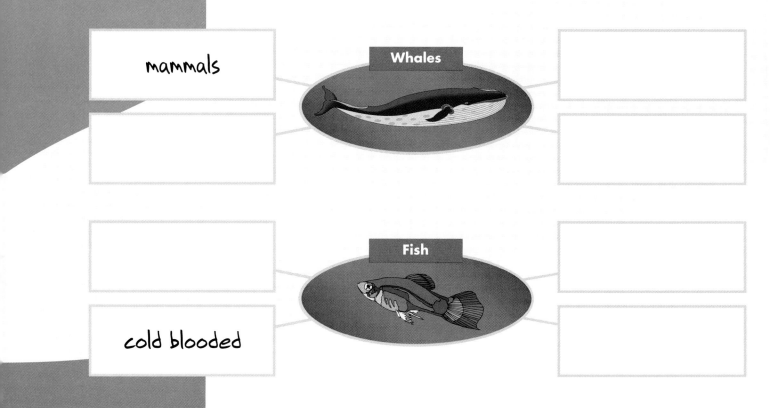

mammals

Whales

cold blooded

Fish

2. About how many kinds of whales are there?

 Ⓐ sixty-two Ⓒ seventy-five

 Ⓑ seventy   Ⓓ eighty

3. Where are you likely to find whales in winter?

 Ⓐ Arctic   Ⓒ warmer waters

 Ⓑ Antarctic Ⓓ colder water

4. We know whales are mammals because they

 Ⓐ gather in larger family groups.

 Ⓑ can stay under water for a long time.

 Ⓒ swim in warm and cold water.

 Ⓓ give birth to live babies.

5. What are baleen whales and toothed whales? Give an example of each type and explain some differences using facts and details from the article.

During winter, whales migrate to warmer water.

_____

_____

_____

_____

_____

_____

_____

_____

Focus on Comparing and Contrasting

★ **When you compare or contrast things, you find out how they are the same and how they are different.**

1. Complete the chart to compare whales (mammals) and fish using the phrases below.

mammal

fish

- need air to breathe
- have live babies
- don't feed their babies
- are warm-blooded
- live in water
- lay eggs
- are cold-blooded
- feed milk to their babies
- don't need air to breathe
- swim with their tails

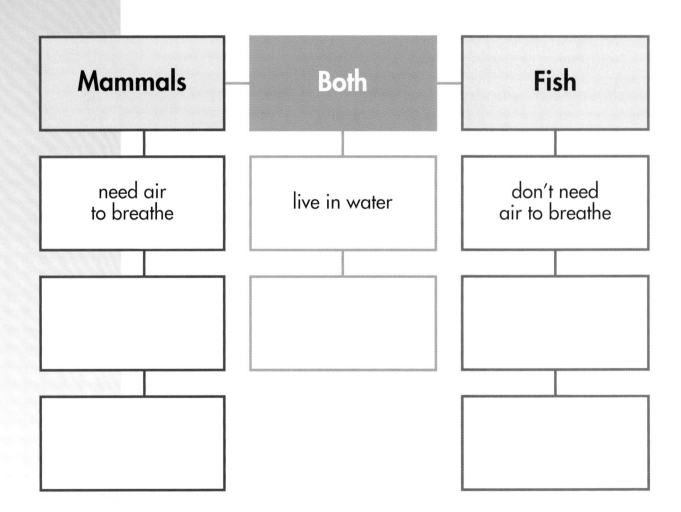

Mammals	Both	Fish
need air to breathe	live in water	don't need air to breathe

Migrating Monarchs

Insects migrate, too. They travel to find warm weather and food. Monarch butterflies may have the long-distance record. These black, yellow, and orange butterflies travel in **swarms** of thousands. They look like black clouds floating in the air. Some monarchs travel from Canada or the nothern United States to Florida, Mexico, and California, where their parent's **journey** began. Sometimes they migrate over 2,000 miles!

2. In the article "Migrating Monarchs," butterfly swarms are compared to

 Ⓐ oranges.   Ⓒ blue skies.

 Ⓑ black clouds.   Ⓓ the yellow sun.

3. Write a sentence or two comparing dolphin herds to swarms of monarchs. Which group has more members? Use facts and details from each story to support your comparison.

_____

_____

_____

_____

_____

Speedy Animals

ad•van•tage
something that can be of extra help or use

slith•er to slide or move along a surface

Birds are the fastest-moving animals in the world. The peregrine falcon can fly 180 miles per hour (mph). The golden eagle flies 120 miles mph. Flying gives birds an **advantage** over other animals.

Land animals and sea animals move very fast, too. The fastest animal on land is the cheetah. Cheetahs can run as fast as seventy mph. In the water, sailfish can swim as fast as a cheetah can run. That is faster than the speed limit for cars in some places.

Can you guess which animal moves the slowest? If you guessed the turtle you are both right and wrong. The land turtle gets the prize for moving slowly. Sea turtles are much faster. They can swim as fast as twenty mph. That is faster than a bat flies through the air, a snake **slithers** across the grass, or a human can swim!

Why are some animals speedy? Eagles and cheetahs are hunters, and need to catch their food. Slow-moving animals like the turtle need a shell for protection since they cannot run fast.

1. How much faster is the peregrine falcon than the golden eagle?

_____

2. Which are the two fastest animals in the world?

Ⓐ falcon and eagle   Ⓒ cheetah and sailfish

Ⓑ falcon and cheetah   Ⓓ cheetah and turtle

3. How does the speed of a sailfish compare to the speed of a sea turtle?

_____

_____

4. Complete the number line to show which animal is the fastest and which animal is the slowest using facts and details from "Speedy Animals."

0 mph	20mph	70 mph	120 mph	180 mph

_____ _____	_____ _____	_____ _____	_____ _____

5. List the creatures that, according to the article, are slower than a sea turtle.

_____

_____

6. Each of the fastest animals on land and in the sky is a hunter. Why do hunters need to run or fly fast? Use facts and details from the story to explain your answer.

_____

_____

_____

_____

This eagle is catching a fish.

Build Your Vocabulary

Answer each question by writing a word or phrase from the box.

migrate	blue whale	bird
baleen	body temperature	mammal

1. What kind of animal gives birth to live babies?

_____

2. What word means "to travel to reach warm weather or food"?

_____

3. Warm-blooded and **cold-blooded** are terms that describe

Ⓐ cheetahs.   Ⓒ body temperature.

Ⓑ fish.   Ⓓ mammals and birds.

4. What are the bony plates in some whale's mouths called?

_____

5. Cross out the word that does not belong with the others.
Write a sentence telling why.

     monarch   falcon   turtle

_____

Did You Know?

Animals that migrate know how to find places. In experiments, scientists take birds away from their migrating path. The "lost" birds can find their way back! List two animals that migrate.

_____

Tornadoes! Airplane crashes! Huge scaly monsters!

How do movie makers create a twisting, turning tornado? Have you ever seen an airplane fall out of the sky? Would you invite a huge scaly monster into your living room? If so, you have started thinking about the magic of movies and television.

In this unit, you will read some stories about making special effects for movies. As you enjoy the thrills, you will discover how the skills of summarizing and comparing and contrasting can help you better understand the inside story of things.

Think About It

Here is a list of jobs involved in movie making. Circle one and write a sentence or two about what a person who has that job does.

director   teacher   actor   electrician

designer   cameraman   computer programmer

_____

_____

Let's Read!

SURPRISES AND SHOCKS

✓ Vocabulary

as•ter•oid a very small planet that travels around the sun

cre•ate to make something by using your imagination

fre•quent•ly common or happening often

(1) **M**onsters leap out of people's stomachs! A huge **asteroid** hits the Earth and sends water gushing everywhere! Where do these kinds of things take place? At the movies, of course. How do these thrilling things happen? To find the answer, let's look at the inside story of making special effects in the movies.

(2) Many people work behind the scenes when a movie is made. Carpenters and metal workers build props, and electricians work with lighting and sound. Artists, puppeteers, computer designers, and programmers all work together. It may require hundreds of people and weeks of work to **create** a scene that lasts a minute or less in the movie.

(3) There are three types of special effects that we **frequently** see in movies: visual effects, physical effects, and makeup effects.

A summary states the most important ideas in a paragraph or article.

React • Summarize

Summarize the second paragraph. Write a phrase or sentence that tells how many kinds of people are needed to create special effects.

_____

_____

(4) **VISUAL EFFECTS** Have you ever seen one actor play twin brothers or sisters? Sometimes, a single actor can play many characters in the same scene! When you see two or three people who look alike, you are probably watching the same actor play different characters on the screen at the same time. This type of visual effect is created by using **multiple** cameras. Visual effects are also created by computers, which can combine pictures that come from different sources. When you watch space aliens climb the Empire State Building, you know that computers have been at work!

(5) **PHYSICAL EFFECTS Enormous** dinosaurs or frightening alien spiders with scary metal teeth that appear on screen are often created using physical effects. A piece of electronic machinery and a small, hand-held puppet may be combined to create a scary or unusual creature that looks huge. Actors and directors must be careful with these puppet-machines; sometimes they break down or get out of control and hurt the actors.

(6) **MAKEUP EFFECTS** Special effects are created using makeup, wigs, and lots and lots of rubber. An actor can be made into a spooky, weird, or funny-looking freak with makeup. Directors need to be careful

✓ **Vocabulary**

mul•ti•ple many, several

e•nor•mous huge, gigantic

"Wow! That could never happen in real life!"

React • Make a Comparison

Complete this sentence in your own words:
A movie with special effects is more interesting to watch than one without because

_____

_____

Vocabulary

suf•fer to feel strongly, to feel uncomfortable or endure.

when they use made-up actors. Sometimes the actor **suffers** from the heat of the stage lights and the weight of the costume.

(7) Special effects make us jump out of our seats. They make us laugh until tears roll down our cheeks. They make us throw our popcorn straight up into the air. Special effects surprise, shock, and tickle us all the way through a movie!

Focus on Summarizing

★ **To list or retell the main events or ideas in a story or article is called summarizing. Before you write a summary sentence, jot down notes about the main idea in each paragraph.**

1. Write some words or phrases about the main idea of the four paragraphs in "Surprises and Shocks."

Paragraph 1: _____

_____

Paragraph 2: _____

_____

Paragraph 3: _____

_____

Paragraph 4: _____

_____

2. Reread paragraph 5. Summarize each sentence.

First Sentence: Enormous dinosaurs or frightening alien spiders with scary metal teeth that appear on screen are often created using physical effects.

My Words: Movie monsters are created with physical effects.

Second Sentence: A piece of electronic machinery and a small, hand-held puppet may be combined to create a scary or unusual creature that looks huge.

My Words:

_____

_____

Third Sentence: Actors and directors must be careful with these puppet-machines; sometimes they break down or get out of control and hurt the actors.

My Words:

_____

_____

3. The final step when you summarize a story is to combine all of your sentences into one. Use the sentences you wrote to create a summary of paragraph 5.

Example Summary: Movie monsters are made with small machines and puppets and can be dangerous.

My Summary:

_____

_____

Focus on Comparing and Contrasting

★ Thinking about how things compare with each other can help you better understand what you read. When you compare and contrast things, you show how they are alike and different.

1. Complete this diagram to show at least one way in which visual and makeup effects are alike and different.

Visual Effects and Makeup Effects	
<u>Alike</u>	<u>Different</u>
Both involve actors.	

2. Complete this diagram to show at least one way in which makeup effects and physical effects are alike and different.

Makeup Effects and Physical Effects	
<u>Alike</u>	<u>Different</u>
	Physical effects use machines. Makeup effects use rubber.

3. List some other ways all special effects are alike.

_____

_____

Godzilla— A Monster for All Time

He was born one night in 1954. He is 50, 80, or 100 **meters** tall, depending on the movie. Godzilla is a giant lizard-monster. His size and strength has won the hearts of theatergoers.

Godzilla has created a great deal of **destruction** in films. He battled a number of bad monsters: Anguirus, Mechagodzilla, and many others. He also crushed the city of Osaka, Japan.

Over the years, Godzilla's look has not changed much. But, if you look closely, there are a few differences. In one movie his tail was lengthened, in another, his body had red patches and his eyes glowed a fiery red.

Whatever physical changes have occurred in Godzilla, one thing has stayed the same. The world continues to love this great big monster.

4. What physical changes have occurred in Godzilla since his birth? List four differences.

   _____

   _____

5. In what ways has Godzilla remained the same throughout his movie career?

   _____

   _____

✔ **Vocabulary**

me•ter a metric unit of measurement, 1 meter = 3.3 feet

de•struc•tion the action of destroying something

Old and New Special Effects

In the past, how would a movie director and his crew create what looked and sounded like a hurricane for a movie? They would use galloping horses to make the noise and blowing fans for the wind. And guess what? A film director and his crew might still use that **method** today!

Now, computers can be used to make **images** and animations come to life on the screen alongside actors. The special effects of today are so believable, they make you think that almost anything can happen.

Fortunately, creating special effects is much safer now. Hollywood stars are no longer asked to risk their lives by jumping on chunks of real ice floating down a real river toward a real waterfall. Today, trained stunt people, rather than the stars themselves, are asked to do dangerous tricks.

1. How have special effects changed over the years? List two ways.

_____

_____

2. How have special effects stayed the same over the years? List two ways.

_____

Vocabulary

meth•od a step-by-step way of doing or creating something

im•age a picture

3. Movie stunts were dangerous in the past because

Ⓐ the actors were braver.

Ⓑ the actors did the stunts themselves.

Ⓒ the directors wanted thrilling stunts.

Ⓓ the audience wanted thrilling stunts.

4. This story is mostly about

Ⓐ dangerous stunts.　　Ⓒ old and new special effects.

Ⓑ brave actors.　　Ⓓ audiences.

5. In the box below, jot down a few notes about the main idea in the first paragraph of "Old and New Special Effects."

Paragraph 1:
_____
_____

6. Write a brief summary of the article "Old and New Special Effects."

_____

_____

_____

_____

_____

_____

Build Your Vocabulary

1. Complete the story using words from the box.

method	create	destruction
hilarious	body	visual

Okay, everybody, it is time to get to work on our exciting, new movie. It is going to be very funny. In fact, it will be **(1)** _____.

The movie is going to have a lot of special physical and **(2)** _____ effects, too. The star is a new monster named Malla. Malla was born at a mall where some atomic accidents took place.

Malla has enormous arms, legs, head, and a big fat **(3)** _____. He will even be bigger than the Empire State Building!

We will use a careful step-by-step **(4)** _____ for filming. To show how the monster can **(5)** _____ so much **(6)** _____, we will use models of cities. Film of the models will be combined with film of real cities to give the movie a realistic feel.

Okay, everybody! Let's get going! We've got a hit on our hands!

Dive! Spin Twirl! Jump

There is nothing quite like adventure high in the sky. Daredevils of the air thrill us with their amazing **feats**. Get ready! You will be on the edge of your seat as you read about these adventurers and their journeys.

In this unit you will read about Brian Jones and Bertrand Piccard's attempt to navigate a hot-air balloon around the world. As you enjoy their adventures, sharpen your skills and strategies as a reader by thinking about cause and effect and summarizing.

✔ Vocabulary

feat a daring deed or action

Think About It

Write a sentence about an exciting time in your life. You might write about a trip or an exciting event.

_____

_____

The World's Greatest Ballooning Adventure

Vocabulary

pro•pane burn•er
a gas fueled flame used to heat air in a hot-air balloon to make it rise

"Look. Over there. Up in the sky!"

As you look out over the treetops, you spot a huge red and yellow hot-air balloon. You hear a whooshing sound as the **propane burner** heats the air in the balloon to make it rise up into the clear morning sky. You wonder what it is like to float over the earth in a balloon.

Ever since 1783, when the Montgolfier (mont-GOLF-ee-ay) brothers launched the first balloon over France, people have been in love with the great adventure of ballooning.

Today, ballooning is still high adventure. There are many exciting journeys to be taken and records to be broken.

A cause is a reason something happens. The effect is what happens.

React • Identify Cause and Effect

What makes the balloon rise?

_____

_____

Did you know that people have tried for many years to fly around the world in a balloon? Balloons can easily be blown off course or crash in bad weather. In fact, no one completed the trip until 1999.

In 1998, a crew of daredevils made a special attempt in a huge balloon that was as tall as the Empire State Building. The crew used helium as fuel. **Helium** took them much higher in the sky than propane, the fuel that is usually used. The balloon went near the **stratosphere** where the weather is calmer. But, a great storm appeared and the balloon crashed ten miles north of the island of Oahu, Hawaii. They were disappointed, but unhurt.

✔ **Vocabulary**

he•li•um a very light gas used for fuel

strat•o•sphere part of the atmosphere, 6-15 miles from the Earth's surface

React • Summarize

What record were the balloonists trying to break?

Ⓐ Flying a hot-air balloon.

Ⓒ Flying an airplane.

Ⓑ Flying around the world.

Ⓓ Flying a kite.

A good summary starts with an important idea or fact.

In 1999, Brian Jones and Bertrand Piccard finally made it all the way in a balloon as tall as the Eiffel Tower. It was powered by propane, and the crew took a chance by steering their balloon far south of Hawaii. In the end, the weather was on their side, and they made it all the way.

Steve Fossett, who had tried five times for the record himself, **congratulated** his rivals saying that theirs was "one of the greatest competitions in **aviation** history."

Focus on Cause and Effect

★ **It is important to understand how one event can cause another event to happen. To find the cause, ask yourself why an event occurred. To find the effect, ask yourself what happened as a result.**

1. Read the following sentence from "The World's Greatest Ballooning Adventure." Complete the cause-effect chart.

You hear a whooshing sound as the propane burner heats the air to make the balloon rise.

Cause (Why)	Effect (What)
The propane burner heats the air. **SO ▶**	_____ _____

2. Read another passage about ballooning. Complete the cause-effect chart below.

Helium took them higher in the sky than other balloons. The balloon went into the stratosphere where the weather is usually calmer.

Cause (Why)	Effect (What)
_____ _____ SO ▶	The balloon went into the stratosphere.

3. Why did Jones and Piccard make it around the world? List two reasons.

_____

_____

_____

_____

4. Why is it hard to fly around the world?

Ⓐ Too many people do it.
Ⓑ The balloons are too big.
Ⓒ It costs too much.
Ⓓ Balloons can blow off course.

5. What was the effect of the storm off the coast of Oahu?

_____

_____

_____

_____

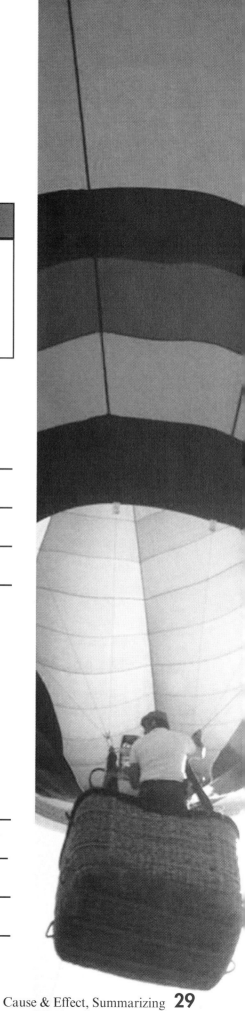

Focus on Summarizing

★ **Summarizing means telling about something using as few words as possible. To summarize, consider what the story or article is mainly about, then write it in your own words.**

1. Think back to the article you read about ballooning. Circle the important details in the story below.

people on the ground	first balloonists
balloonists break records	ballooning around the world
balloon festivals	helium balloons

2. Reread each paragraph in the article. In the space provided, write the main ideas of three different paragraphs that you feel are important in the article. Then combine the main ideas to write a summary.

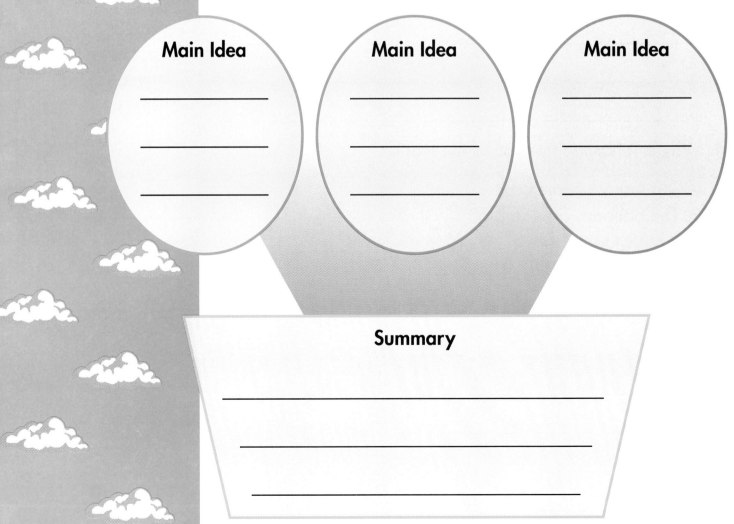

Main Idea

_____

_____

_____

Main Idea

_____

_____

_____

Main Idea

_____

_____

_____

Summary

_____

_____

_____

Sky Diver's Amazing Escape

Roger Reynolds was scared. He was seventeen and taking his first **skydiving** class. Roger held his breath. He jumped from the small plane. He steered himself to a safe landing.

After that, Roger was hooked and skydived almost once a week. When he graduated, Roger joined the Army and became a Green Beret. Roger was so good that he was asked to join the Golden Knights, the Army **Exhibition** Parachute Team.

Roger performed with the team many times. Then, on Roger's nine-hundred-fifty-ninth jump, something awful happened. Roger's parachute did not open. He fell 2,800 feet and hit the ground at eighty-five miles per hour.

He was still alive! But, Roger broke every major bone in his body. Doctors did not think he would walk again, but Roger never gave up. He exercised and even studied medicine to find a way to heal himself. Then, Roger Reynolds decided to be a doctor.

3. Write a sentence to summarize Roger Reynolds' adventure.

_____

_____

4. Read each sentence in the summary below. Number the sentences so the summary makes sense.

_____ Because of his injuries he became a doctor.

_____ Roger Reynolds learned to skydive at seventeen.

_____ After many jumps he had a bad accident.

_____ He was so good he joined the Golden Knights.

Vocabulary

sky•div•ing the sport of jumping from an airplane with a parachute to land safely

ex•hi•bi•tion a public demonstration

Flying with the Birds

Vocabulary

hang gli•der a large kite that a person uses to glide in the air

trap•eze bar a short crossbar used to control the flight of a hang glider

How would you like to soar high in the air like a bird? **Hang glider** pilots do just that. They use a wing, like a large kite, to drift on air currents. Glider pilots can dive and turn as easily as a bird.

Taking off in a hang glider is as easy as running. The pilot runs into the wind and pushes forward on the **trapeze bar** so that the nose of the hang glider kite will lift upward. This allows air to fill the glider's wing. Suddenly the glider lifts off the ground to glide in the sky.

When the pilot wants to land, the pilot pulls the trapeze bar down. The hang glider acts like a parachute. It catches the air, slows the hang glider down, and gently drops the pilot to the ground.

1. Summarize the steps involved for a hang glider to take off.

_____

_____

2. How does the trapeze bar cause the hang glider to lift into the air?

_____

_____

3. Which is the best summary of how a pilot lands a hang glider?

   Ⓐ The pilot lets go of the trapeze bar.
   Ⓑ The pilot pulls the trapeze bar down.
   Ⓒ The pilot runs into the wind.
   Ⓓ The pilot pushes the trapeze bar forward.

4. Write a sentence to summarize the main idea of this article.

_____

_____

5. Read the following sentences about hang gliding. Complete the cause-effect chart.

    When the pilot wants to land, the pilot pulls the trapeze bar down. The hang glider acts like a parachute. It catches the air, slows the hang glider down, and gently drops the pilot to the ground.

Cause (Why)	Effect (What)
The pilot pulls the trapeze bar down. **SO** ▶	_____ _____

Build Your Vocabulary

Answer each question or finish each sentence by writing a word from the box.

helium	sky diver	hang glider	survived
congratulate	stratosphere	trapeze bar	propane

1. Which two words name gases or fuels?

   _____

2. Which word describes a person who parachutes from an airplane? _____

3. A hang glider's _____ helps it take off and land.

4. Roger Reynolds _____ a parachute fall.

5. Which word below is not a synonym for exhibition?

   Ⓐ show   Ⓒ impair

   Ⓑ appearance   Ⓓ display

6. Congratulate means

   Ⓐ to come together.
   Ⓑ to mix up or confuse.
   Ⓒ to tell someone that you are happy for her or his success.
   Ⓓ to have a strong belief or trust in someone.

Did You Know?

The terms **hang glider** and **sky diver** use more than one word to describe a person or object. The terms **race car driver** and **horseback rider** do the same thing. List some other similar terms.

_____

_____

Part A

Read the selection below. Use the skills you have learned to answer the questions, choose the best answers, or complete the sentences.

Captured by a Narrative

You bite your lip. You squirm in your seat. Your heart is pounding. Your mother calls you for dinner, but you keep on reading. You can not put your book down. You must find out what happens next. You keep reading . . .

The night was stormy and dark. The bus, packed with third and fourth graders coming home from camp, clung to the edge of the narrow road. It twisted its way down the steep mountainside. Suddenly, brakes screeched, the bus jerked sideways, and Jack saw the edge of the cliff . . .

A good story like this can really grab you! Most writing that captures your attention like this is a narrative. A narrative is a type of writing that tells a story. The events in a narrative are often told in time sequence, or the order in which things happened. One event in a story may cause another to occur.

Facts and Details

1. Which word is another word for **story**?

   Ⓐ narrative   Ⓒ event

   Ⓑ sequence   Ⓓ style

Comparing and Contrasting

2. Which statement tells how the first and third paragraphs are different?

   Ⓐ One describes an effect and the other gives a definition.

   Ⓑ One gives an example and the other describes different writing styles.

   Ⓒ One tells what happens first and the other tells what happens next.

   Ⓓ One is real and the other is make believe.

Cause and Effect

3. Which word from the selection best describes the effect of reading a good survival story?

   Ⓐ pounding   Ⓒ interesting

   Ⓑ narrative   Ⓓ captures

Summarizing

4. Write a sentence or two describing what a good survival story is like.

_____

_____

5. Reread the narrative example. Write a few sentences telling what happens next.

_____

_____

Part B

Read the selection below. Use the skills you have learned to answer the questions, choose the best answers, or complete the sentences.

The Survivor Tree

The slippery elm tree grew in the middle of a parking lot. It was a volunteer seed, a plant that had grown from a wind-blown seed. For years, water ran off the asphalt and did not soak into the ground. So, the elm had spread its roots wide and **shallow,** to collect any water it could. Still, the tree grew, and was now sixty years old.

Rumors say that George Washington's troops boiled slippery elm branches to make soup to help them survive a harsh winter. But, no one made soup out of this tree in Oklahoma City.

The Alfred P. Murrah Federal Building was nearby. At 9:02 A.M. on April 19, 1995, a bomb exploded in front of the Murrah Building. The blast **scorched** the elm's branches. All its leaves were blown away. **Debris** filled the branches. Inside the building, 168 people died. Somehow the elm survived the blast. People began calling it the Survivor Tree.

The Oklahoma Department of Agriculture worried that it might die, and sent Mark Bays, a forester, to treat the tree. Bays and others picked the debris out of the Survivor Tree's branches. They trimmed deadwood. They **chiseled** the asphalt away from the elm's roots, leaving a bed in the shape of the state of Oklahoma. Then, they added plant food and the tree showed signs that it would live.

✓ **Vocabulary**

shal•low not very deep

scorched burned the surface

de•bris the remains of something destroyed or broken down

chis•eled cut

Bays and others wanted to save the tree. Their first step was to harvest the elm's seeds and try to grow them. Foresters also cut 100 shoots from the elm's branches. If the seeds grew, the Survivor Tree would be a parent to the new trees. If the shoots or cuttings grew, the new trees would be exact copies of the Survivor Tree.

When a memorial service was held the next year, 400 saplings had grown from the elm's seeds. Agriculture officials handed out those saplings to survivors of the blast and families of victims. The Survivor Tree stood for the ruggedness of Oklahoma's people, endurance, and hope. Hope would live on in Oklahoma City.

Facts and Details

1. What did the blast do to the tree?

    Ⓐ harvested it   Ⓒ scorched it

    Ⓑ soaked it   Ⓓ killed it

Compare and Contrast

2. How are George Washington's tree and the Survivor Tree alike?

    Ⓐ both slippery elms   Ⓒ both damaged by fire

    Ⓑ both used as food   Ⓓ both grew in Oklahoma

Cause and Effect

3. Draw lines to match each cause to its effect.

Cause	Effect
• boiled elm branches	• elm spread its roots
• blast at the Murrah Building	• soldiers survived a harsh winter
• water did not soak in	• slippery elm grew in parking lot
• a volunteer seed	• elm's branches were scorched

Start with What You Know

At the end of 1998, Russia and the United States launched into space the first phase of a new space station. These two countries once competed in a "space race." Now they are working together with other countries to build an International Space Station.

The new space station will be a marvel. It will be larger than a football field and have millions of parts. It will cost billions of dollars. Once complete, scientists from around the world will be living and doing experiments on board, year round.

In this unit, you will read reports or stories about the International Space Station. As you learn more about the space station, you will learn how to find the main idea of an article and practice making predictions.

Think About It
List some things that would be very difficult to do without gravity.

_____

_____

_____

LIVING WITH THE STARS

Since the dawn of time, people have looked up at the stars. Before long, people will live among them. In December 1998, the United States and Russia launched into space the first two pieces of the International Space Station.

When completed, the International Space Station will be made up of millions of parts combined to form dozens of giant **modules**. Astronauts will have to spend about 1,800 hours in space walks trying to assemble the station. It is expected to take more than five years to build. The first crew will consist of three people—an American and two Russians. Later, astronaut crews will come from all over the world to work in the space station.

✔ **Vocabulary**

mod•ule one of a series of units that can be arranged in various ways

A good title tells the main, or most important idea in the story

React • Find the Main Idea

Write another good title for this story.

_____

_____

The **massive** space station will be longer than a football field, and wider than two football fields. There will be the same amount of space on the inside as in a 747 jumbo jet. The space station will be so big that we should be able to see it fly overhead in the night sky.

Special tools and talents are required to assemble the station. The astronauts will have to wear special spacesuits when they go out of the station so that they do not die from a lack of air or **exposure** to extreme temperatures. They will also need to use tools designed for space.

For things that astronauts will not be able to do by themselves, they will get a hand from the Canadians. Actually, they will get a whole arm from Canada—a robotic arm. This robotic arm called the "Canada Hand" is fifty-five feet long and will be able to manipulate objects weighing up to 125 tons.

React • Make a Prediction

How could the robotic arm be used to help assemble the space station?

_____

_____

The main use of the station will be science. There will be dozens of **laboratories** on the station to **conduct** science experiments. In fact, there is even a platform on the outside of a module to be built by the Japanese on which experiments can be exposed to space.

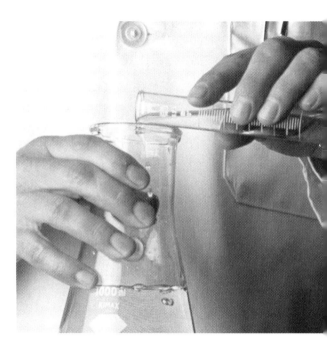

Would you like to go the space station? There is room on the station for seven scientists at a time. One day, you may get to be one of those scientists.

Focus on Main Idea

★ **The main idea is what a report or article is mainly about. Sometimes one sentence in a paragraph states the main idea. The other sentences tell more about it.**

1. Read the first paragraph on this page. Choose the sentence that states the main idea and write it on the lines below.

_____

_____

2. Write a phrase or sentence from the paragraph telling more about the main idea.

_____

_____

3. Read the following paragraph. Complete the word web to include supporting details.

When completed, the International Space Station will be made up of millions of parts combined to form dozens of giant modules. Astronauts will have to spend about 1,800 hours in space walks trying to assemble the station. It is expected to take more than five years to build. The first crew will consist of three people—an American and two Russians. Later, astronaut crews will come from all over the world to work in the space station.

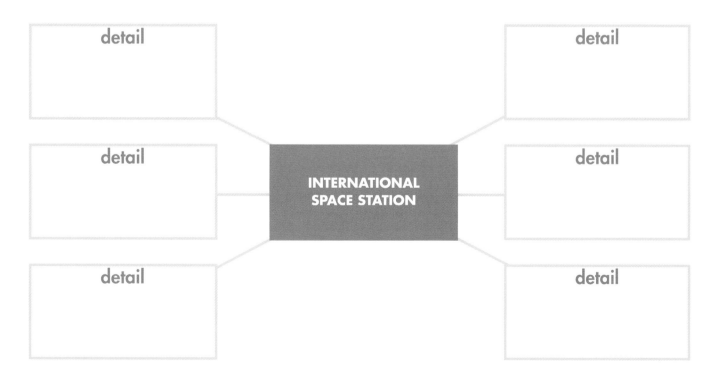

detail		detail
detail	INTERNATIONAL SPACE STATION	detail
detail		detail

Focus on Making Predictions

Gravity Gets You Every Time

If you jump in the air, you will fall back to Earth. Why? Gravity. No matter how much you try, it is difficult to escape the pull of **gravity**. The effect of gravity pulling down on us gives us our weight. Other planets that are smaller than Earth have weaker gravity pulls, so we would weigh less on them. On a larger planet we would weigh more.

Getting to the space station 100 miles above Earth will not be easy. The space shuttle will have to fly very fast to escape the pull of gravity. Gravity exerts a force on objects near each other. When you drop a rock, it falls toward the center of the Earth. As it falls, it goes faster. Air may slow it down a little, but in space, where there is a **vacuum**, there is no air to slow it down.

As the space station orbits, gravity pulls it. To keep gravity from pulling the space station toward Earth, it needs to fly at a little more than 25,000 miles per hour. If it flies much faster, it could get so far away from Earth that it escapes Earth's gravity. Objects that are not close to other objects are not affected by gravity. They weigh nothing and can just float around in space.

★ **Predicting helps us use the information we read to understand what might happen in the future.**

1. If the space station flew at 20,000 miles per hour it would

    Ⓐ fall to Earth.   Ⓒ reach the Moon.

    Ⓑ fly toward the Sun.   Ⓓ never take off.

✓ Vocabulary

grav•i•ty the force of attraction on Earth and on other planets

vac•uum a volume that has no air, or less air inside than outside

2. Write a phrase or sentence telling what would happen if the orbiting space station suddenly started to fly at 50,000 mph.

_____

3. Here is a list of some objects in our solar system. Review the list and complete the chart that follows.

Bigger than Earth

Jupiter

Neptune

Saturn

Sun

Uranus

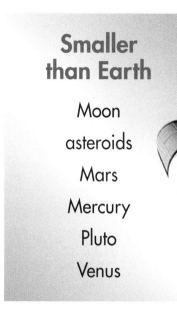

Smaller than Earth

Moon

asteroids

Mars

Mercury

Pluto

Venus

If you visit . . .	What will happen to your weight?	Why?
Jupiter	It will increase.	The pull of gravity will be stronger.
Pluto		
Moon		
Sun		
Venus		
an asteroid		

Space Station Science Gels into Amazing Products

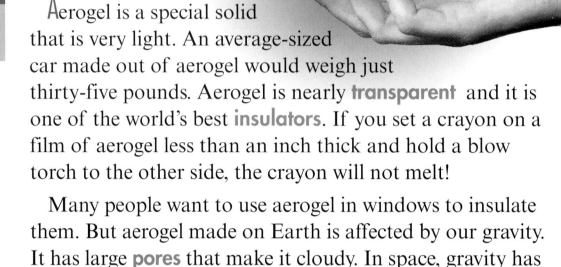

Vocabulary

trans•par•ent
clear, easy to see through

in•su•la•tor
keeps something cold or hot

pores openings in a substance such as skin

Aerogel is a special solid that is very light. An average-sized car made out of aerogel would weigh just thirty-five pounds. Aerogel is nearly **transparent** and it is one of the world's best **insulators**. If you set a crayon on a film of aerogel less than an inch thick and hold a blow torch to the other side, the crayon will not melt!

Many people want to use aerogel in windows to insulate them. But aerogel made on Earth is affected by our gravity. It has large **pores** that make it cloudy. In space, gravity has no effect on aerogel and the pores are many times smaller. That means the gel is less cloudy and more usable.

Aerogel is one example of a product that can be made in space and possibly used here on Earth.

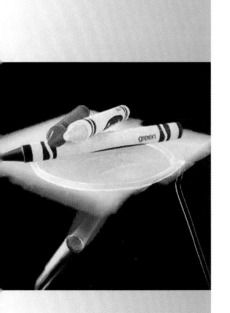

1. Which sentence best describes the main idea?

  Ⓐ Aerogel is a good insulator.

  Ⓑ Aerogel is a new kind of product that can only be made in space.

  Ⓒ Aerogel has large pores that make it cloudy on Earth.

  Ⓓ Aerogel is a good surface to use for cooking.

2. Which is not a detail that supports the main idea?

  Ⓐ Aerogel is affected by gravity.

  Ⓑ In space, aerogel is not affected by gravity.

  Ⓒ Aerogel is less cloudy when made in space.

  Ⓓ You can make an average-size car out of aerogel.

3. For each main idea, write details that support it.

"Aerogel has many amazing properties."

_____

_____

_____

"Aerogel is better when made in space."

_____

_____

_____

4. Think of two ways that aerogel might be used in your home. You might consider aerogel made on Earth for some things, and aerogel made in space for others. Explain why aerogel is a good product.

_____

_____

"What could I make out of aerogel?"

5. If you wanted to find out more about aerogel, where might you look? Whom might you ask? Write a sentence about where you might find the most information.

_____

_____

Build Your Vocabulary

Answer each question and complete each sentence by writing a word from the box.

modules	massive	exposure	gravity
conduct	transparent	insulator	pores

1. If you can see through something, it is _____ .

2. A substance that prevents heat from passing through it is an _____ .

3. There will be dozens of _____ in the new space station.

4. If you suck all the air out of a jar, what will you create?

Ⓐ a vacuum   Ⓒ a full jar

Ⓑ an empty jar   Ⓓ a headache

5. Write a sentence that uses the following two words.

vacuum/exposure

_____

_____

6. Which of the following words is an antonym of massive?

Ⓐ huge   Ⓑ vast   Ⓒ grand   Ⓓ miniature

Did You Know?

Long ago, people used the stars to find their way around. Depending on where in the sky the stars were, they knew where they were on Earth. Write the name of a star you know.

_____

Start with What You Know

Amazing Kids

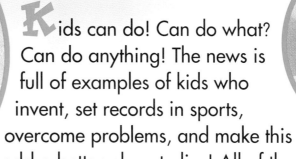

Kids can do! Can do what? Can do anything! The news is full of examples of kids who invent, set records in sports, overcome problems, and make this world a better place to live! All of these kids have something in **common**. They are truly **remarkable** kids with truly amazing stories!

In this unit, you will read some short, nonfiction articles about the amazing lives and contributions of a number of boys and girls. As you read, you will make inferences about what you have read. You will also pay close attention to recalling facts and details to help you to remember the important parts of each person's life and story.

✓ **Vocabulary**

com•mon shared by two or more people

re•mark•a•ble worth noticing

qual•i•ty a special characteristic of someone

Think About It
What makes someone amazing? Write a list of **qualities** that you think make someone special.

_____

_____

_____

Kids Can!

Sometimes, it seems that the history of the world is only about grown-ups. But you may discover that the history of the world is also made up of the achievements of amazing kids!

What is an "amazing kid"? Keep that question in mind as you read about the following young people from the past and present.

Nadia Comaneci (co-man-EETCH) from Romania, became the first athlete in any women's Olympic gymnastic event to score a perfect 10! She won that score for her performance on the uneven parallel bars. She went on to win three gold medals and one silver medal at the 1976 Olympics and score seven perfect tens.

Nadia was only 14 years old when she **astonished** the world with her **accomplishment**. Several other women gymnasts won perfect tens in the 1976 Olympics. But Nadia, younger and smaller than her teammates, won the hearts of the public.

✓ Vocabulary

as•ton•ish to make someone feel very surprised

ac•com•plish•ment an achievement

Use clues in the article and what you already know to make an inference about what is not stated.

React • Make an Inference

Use facts and details from the story to make an inference. Why was Nadia amazing to people?

_____

_____

Here are some more amazing kids from history.

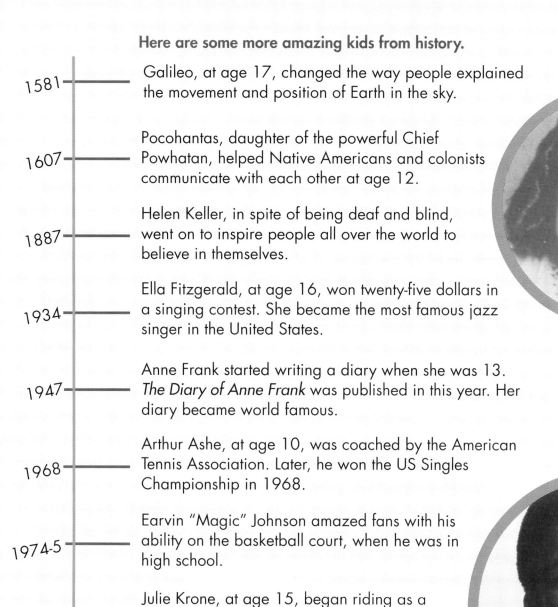

1581 — Galileo, at age 17, changed the way people explained the movement and position of Earth in the sky.

1607 — Pocohantas, daughter of the powerful Chief Powhatan, helped Native Americans and colonists communicate with each other at age 12.

1887 — Helen Keller, in spite of being deaf and blind, went on to inspire people all over the world to believe in themselves.

1934 — Ella Fitzgerald, at age 16, won twenty-five dollars in a singing contest. She became the most famous jazz singer in the United States.

1947 — Anne Frank started writing a diary when she was 13. *The Diary of Anne Frank* was published in this year. Her diary became world famous.

1968 — Arthur Ashe, at age 10, was coached by the American Tennis Association. Later, he won the US Singles Championship in 1968.

1974-5 — Earvin "Magic" Johnson amazed fans with his ability on the basketball court, when he was in high school.

1979 — Julie Krone, at age 15, began riding as a professional jockey. She helped open up possibilities for women as jockeys.

1991 — Diana Golden, at age 12, lost one of her legs in an accident. With great determination, she bravely proved that one-legged skiing is possible.

Anne Frank

Earvin "Magic" Johnson

React • Find Facts and Details

Find facts and details about these amazing kids in the timeline. Who is the youngest amazing kid in the time line?

Ⓐ Julie Krone   Ⓒ Anne Frank

Ⓑ Helen Keller   Ⓓ Earvin Johnson

Zlata Filipovic (fee-LEE-poh-vic) is famous for writing a diary. *Zlata's Diary: A Child's Life in Sarajevo* tells about a war that took place in and around her home town of Sarajevo, in what was once the country of Yugoslavia.

Zlata started her diary in 1991, just before her eleventh birthday. In her diary, Zlata talks about her fears and hopes for life after the war. Zlata's diary is a favorite book of children all around the world.

Focus on Making Inferences

★ **Sometimes a writer leaves clues to help you form your own ideas about the article. These clues help you to read between the lines. To infer what the author does not tell you, think about your own experiences and look for clues.**

1. Read these sentences from "Kids Can!" Answer the question by completing the chart.

Several other women gymnasts won perfect tens in the 1976 Olympics. But Nadia, younger and smaller than her teammates, won the hearts of the public.

Why did Nadia win the hearts of the public?

Writer tells...		I know...		I infer...
Other gymnasts got 10s, but Nadia was young and small.	+	People like to see little kids win.	=	The public liked her especially well because ... _____ _____ _____

2. Read these sentences from "Kids Can!" Answer the question by completing the chart.

Zlata started her diary in 1991, just before her eleventh birthday. Zlata's diary is a favorite book of children all around the world.

Why do you think *Zlata's Diary* has become a favorite book?

Writer tells...	I know...	I infer...
Zlata's diary is about her life at age 11.	Kids can relate to other kids' lives.	Kids love her book because ... _____ _____ _____ _____

(with **+** between first two columns and **=** before third column)

3. Read this sentence about Zlata. Complete the chart by making an inference about Zlata.

In her diary Zlata talks about her fears and hopes for life after the war.

Why do you think Zlata wrote her diary?

Writer tells...	I know...	I infer...
Zlata writes about . . . _____ _____ _____	She lived in a place that made her feel... _____ _____ _____	Writing helped her . . . _____ _____ _____

(with **+** between first two columns and **=** before third column)

Focus on Facts and Details

Sometimes tests ask you to find facts and details in a chart or article. Here are some steps to follow when looking for facts and details.

★ Figure out what fact or detail you need.

★ Scan headings and key words for the information.

★ Read carefully to find the fact or detail.

★ Use the fact or detail to answer the question.

1. How old was Diana Golden when she lost her leg? How did she lose her leg? _____

_____

2. In which year did Julie Krone ride in her first race as a jockey?

Ⓐ 1980   Ⓑ 1967   Ⓒ 1975   Ⓓ 1979

3. When did Magic Johnson first get his nickname?

_____

_____

4. Why is Arthur Ashe an "amazing kid"? _____

_____

5. Helen Keller was _____

_____

_____

6. Whose daughter was Pocohantas? Why is she an "amazing kid"? _____

_____

_____

Tiger Woods: A Golf Champion

Who is Tiger Woods? Tiger is a **professional** golfer. He won the Masters Tournament in Augusta, Georgia, in 1997 when he was only 21 years old! Tiger was the first African-Asian American to win the Masters.

When Tiger was less than 2 years old, he began lots of practice at home with his dad. This dedication led to his later success.

Tiger's first major victory came when he was 8 years old. In 1984, Tiger won his first junior world tournament in San Diego, California. During his teenage years, Tiger won many **championships**. When he was 18, he became the youngest golfer to win the United States Amateur Tournament.

Where will his career take Tiger? No one knows. But he might become one of the greatest golfers who ever played the game.

✓ Vocabulary

pro•fes•sion•al a trained specialist

cham•pi•on•ship a competition

7. Tiger Woods is described as _____.

8. Read the following sentences and choose the phrase that best describes how they are related.

During his teenage years, Tiger won many championships. When he was 18, he became the youngest golfer to win the United States Amateur Tournament.

Ⓐ sequence   Ⓑ statement and example

Where will his career take Tiger? No one knows. But he might become one of the greatest golfers who ever played the game.

Ⓐ sequence   Ⓑ fact and opinion

THE BOY WHO LOVED MUSIC

Wolfgang Amadeus Mozart was born in 1756. He was a true musical child **prodigy** from the age of 4 years old.

In 1762, when Mozart was almost 6 years old, his father took his sister and young Mozart to Munich, Germany. Mozart played the **clavichord**. He was a tremendous success. Soon, they took Mozart to perform before the Emperor in Vienna, Austria. The Emperor was delighted with Mozart and called him "the little wizard."

As their fame grew, the Mozart family went on a tour to many countries. The family returned home when Mozart was 10 years old. By then, Mozart was famous throughout Europe.

Over 200 years later, his music is still loved. Mozart will be remembered as a "little **wizard**"—an amazing child!

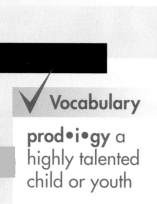

Vocabulary

prod•i•gy a highly talented child or youth

clav•i•chord an early keyboard instrument like a piano

wiz•ard a skillful person

1. How old was Mozart when he returned from the tour that made him famous? _____

2. Mozart was born in

 Ⓐ 1777. Ⓑ 1789. Ⓒ 1756. Ⓓ 1745.

3. What did the Emperor call Mozart?

_____

4. You can infer from the nickname " the little wizard" that the Emperor thought Mozart was

    Ⓐ a success.

    Ⓑ magical.

    Ⓒ quite small.

    Ⓓ unusually gifted.

5. How old was Mozart when he first played music?

    Ⓐ 3 years

    Ⓑ 4 years

    Ⓒ 5 years

    Ⓓ 6 years

6. Think about Mozart's story. Why do you think his father took him to perform before the Emperor?

Writer tells...		I know...		I infer...
_____		_____		_____
_____		_____		_____
_____	+	_____	=	_____
_____		_____		_____
_____		_____		_____
_____		_____		_____

7. Choose a favorite amazing kid from one of the articles. Complete the facts and details web about this amazing kid.

Build Your Vocabulary

Answer each question by writing a word from the box.

prodigy	determination	championship
professional	wizard	accomplishment

1. Which word means "a trained specialist"?

_____

2. Write a sentence to describe a sports team's great success using one or more of the words.

_____

3. Which word is an antonym for achievement?

  Ⓐ success   Ⓒ failure

  Ⓑ triumph   Ⓓ completion

4. Use your answer to question 3 in a sentence.

_____

5. Write a question you would ask one of the amazing kids in the articles. Use one or more of the words in the box in your question. _____

_____

Did You Know?

When a word ends in **-ment**, the word is a noun and is often related to an action. For example, the word **accomplishment** is a noun that means "the act of accomplishing something." Write a list of words you know that end in **-ment** and are nouns.

_____

"Attention on board:

You are about to arrive at Ellis Island."

Why do so many people from all over the world come to live in the United States? How do they get here? Which countries do they come from? Did your great-grandparents come to this country from another place? What did they see when they first **arrived**? What did they bring with them?

For many people, Ellis Island and the Statue of Liberty were the first things people saw when they got to the United States of America. In this unit, you will read three personal histories of people who came to Ellis Island. You will find the main idea in each story and learn how people began their new lives in the United States. You will see how their lives were both similar and different from your own.

 **Vocabulary**

ar•rive to reach a destination or place

Think About It

Do you know anyone who was born in another country? Name another country and write a sentence telling something you know about it.

_____

_____

_____

COMING TO AMERICA

The ship rocked in huge waves. Hundreds of people, jammed into the belly of the ship, felt sick. But they looked forward to what the future held in a new country. In the late 1800s and early 1900s, millions of people sailed to the United States from all over the world. They came not knowing if they could stay in America.

Immigrants sailed on many ships from countries around the world. People **yearned** for a new life. Some looked for freedom. Some looked for a chance to make money and take care of their families. Some wanted to work at jobs they could not hold in their own countries.

Every immigrant who sailed into New York harbor had to go to the Ellis Island immigration **processing** station. The government decided if an immigrant was allowed to stay in the United States. The journey to a new life was not an easy one.

Vocabulary

im•mi•grant a person who leaves one country to settle in another

yearned longed (for), wanted very much

proc•ess•ing to put steps of a procedure into action; to prepare

The main idea is what the article is about. Details help you understand the main idea.

React • Find the Main Idea

Which sentence in the first paragraph best states the main idea of the paragraph? Write it on the line below.

_____

_____

Millions of immigrants arrived at Ellis Island. The buildings on Ellis Island were small and crammed with thousands of people each day. Most people did not speak English. They were excited and happy. But at the same time, they were confused and frightened. They knew that, if they were allowed to stay in America, they might never again see family members left behind.

Doctors and nurses examined the immigrants. The immigrants took a **literacy** test. They waited for hours and hours to go through the processing necessary to enter the United States. Sometimes, they were kept on the island for days, waiting to find out if they would be able to stay.

Not all of the people who came to Ellis Island were allowed to stay. Some people were turned away because of **quotas**. Only a certain number of people were allowed to stay from each country. Can you imagine sailing for weeks, feeling seasick and frightened, only to learn you had to go back home?

✔ **Vocabulary**

lit•er•a•cy the ability to read and write

quo•ta the number admitted

When you compare, look for things that are alike and different.

React • Make a Comparison

Write a sentence comparing an immigrant's experience on the ship to his or her experience on Ellis Island.

_____

_____

Some people were turned away because they could not read or write. Some were turned away due to ailments. Doctors said they were not well. Sometimes, mistakes were made.

Focus on Main Idea

★ **The most important idea in a paragraph or article is called the main idea. Good writers provide supporting facts and details that explain more about the main idea.**

1. Write M for main idea and S for supporting details.

_____ Every immigrant who sailed into New York harbor had to go to Ellis Island.

_____ Hundreds of people, jammed into the belly of the ship, felt sick.

_____ Millions of immigrants arrived at Ellis Island.

_____ Most people did not speak English.

2. The story "Coming to America" is mostly about the experience of

   Ⓐ immigrants.   Ⓒ the reader.

   Ⓑ the author.   Ⓓ everyone.

3. Reread "Coming to America." Complete the web to show supporting details for the main idea.

The journey to America was not easy.

4. Write a sentence about the article "Coming to America"

Focus on Comparing and Contrasting

★ **Looking for comparisons can help you understand an author's ideas. You can see how an author thinks two or more things are alike and different. Words such as *like*, *same*, *as*, *but*, *however*, and *unlike* can be clues when looking for comparisons.**

1. Find a comparison or contrasting statement from "Coming to America" for each sentence below.

   Ⓐ Hundreds of people, jammed into the belly of the ship, felt sick. _____

   _____

   Ⓑ They were excited and happy. _____

   _____

2. Write a sentence comparing and contrasting the reasons that immigrants wanted to come to the United States.

   _____

   _____

3. Compare and contrast the journey that the immigrants took on the ship to a journey you have taken.

Immigrants' Trip   Similarities   My Trip

DOORS CLOSED

In 1923, Molik Sogoian (so-goi-AN) sailed from Armenia to America with his son and other members of his family. They wanted to **pursue** opportunities in this new land. But quotas **thwarted** them. Too many people from Sogoian's country of Armenia had already come to the United States. No more were allowed for the rest of the year.

While the family was awaiting entry into America, a baby girl was born to Sogoian's brother and sister-in-law at Ellis Island. They named her Ellis. Ellis would be allowed to stay. Anyone born in the United States could stay in the country.

Sadly, others in the family, including Sogoian, could not stay in America. So the whole family sailed back to Armenia.

4. How was baby Ellis's experience at Ellis Island different from Molik's?

   Ⓐ Baby Ellis was born in the US and could stay.

   Ⓑ Baby Ellis was born in the US and could not stay.

   Ⓒ Baby Ellis was born to Molik's brother so he could stay.

   Ⓓ Baby Ellis was born in Armenia so she could stay.

5. Molik Sogoian left Armenia with a plan. Compare and contrast what Molik planned with what really happened.

What was planned	What really happened

✔ **Vocabulary**

pur•sue to look for; to follow

thwart•ed to stop from happening; to block

Patrick Shea's Story

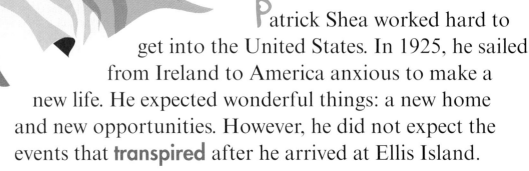

Patrick Shea worked hard to get into the United States. In 1925, he sailed from Ireland to America anxious to make a new life. He expected wonderful things: a new home and new opportunities. However, he did not expect the events that **transpired** after he arrived at Ellis Island.

Doctors told Shea he was sick, that he had only two weeks to live. Shea could not stay in America if he was sick. He was sent back to Ireland.

But in Ireland, doctors said Shea was well. Shea moved to England, where life was better. Then, he **emigrated** from England to Canada.

Finally, Shea returned to America with doctors' notes proving that he was well. He was finally allowed to stay and begin his new life.

 **Vocabulary**

tran•spired
happened

em•i•grat•ed left
one country to
settle in another

1. Which sentence best describes the main idea?

   Ⓐ Patrick Shea wanted a new car.

   Ⓑ Patrick Shea wanted to live in Canada.

   Ⓒ Patrick Shea was not ill when he went to America.

   Ⓓ People who were ill were not allowed to immigrate to America.

2. Which detail supports the main idea?

   Ⓐ Shea could not stay in America.

   Ⓑ Doctors told Shea he was sick.

   Ⓒ Shea worked hard to get to America.

   Ⓓ Shea moved to England.

3. Find a comparison or contrasting statement from "Patrick Shea's Story" for the sentence below. Write it on the lines.

Doctors told Shea he was sick.

_____

_____

_____

4. Compare and contrast Patrick Shea's expectations about the United States. Complete the chart with what you have learned in the story.

What Shea Expected	What Happened
_____	_____
_____	_____
_____	_____
_____	_____

5. In this unit, you have read about immigrants coming to America. What was the most surprising about the experience of people coming to this country? Write a few sentences to compare your feelings about immigrants before you read this unit to how you feel right now.

_____

_____

_____

_____

_____

Build Your Vocabulary

Answer each question by writing a word from the box.

ailments	yearn	processed	emigrate

1. What were the immigrants at Ellis Island tested for?

_____

2. Which word means to leave one country to settle in another? _____

_____

3. Which word describes a feeling of wanting something very much? _____

_____

4. Which word describes what happened to people when they came to Ellis Island? Use it in a sentence.

_____

_____

5. Two of the three words below belong together. Circle the two words and explain why.

       ailments   learn   literacy

_____

Did You Know?

More than 16 million immigrants passed through Ellis Island to live in the United States. Did any of your family come from another country? Which country? Why did they come?

_____

_____

Part A

Read the selection below. Use the skills you have learned to answer the questions, choose the best answers, or complete the sentences.

Fossil Hunting

✓ **Vocabulary**

rock hound a person who looks for rocks

fos•sil the remains of plants or animals, often bones or imprints are fossils

im•print the shape of something pressed into another material

skel•e•ton the bones of a body, a framework

The Rockfinders are a group of dedicated **rock hounds**. They dig for **fossils**, the remains of ancient life. They know a hillside where they have already found many fossils in a layer of sandstone.

The first step in finding fossils is looking in the right place. Each layer of rock in the hillside is from a different time period, long ago. The layer they want is sand that has been pressed into rock. This hard sandstone breaks off in thin pieces.

To find a fossil, the Rockfinders have to look hard. They pick up one rock at a time. With special rock hammers, they hit each piece of sandstone on its thin edge. The layers of the rock crack open like an old sandwich. Sometimes there are **imprints** of underwater plants inside. Sometimes there is the **skeleton** of a fish.

Searching for fossils is like being an explorer. It is exciting. No one knows what is inside each rock. The Rockfinders have found a fossil fish! They are the first people in the world ever to have seen this fish!

Main Idea

1. Which sentence from the selection best states the main idea?

   Ⓐ The Rockfinders are a group of dedicated **rock hounds**.

   Ⓑ To find a **fossil**, the Rockfinders have to look hard.

   Ⓒ Sometimes there is a **skeleton** of a fish.

   Ⓓ They are the first people in the world ever to have seen this fish.

Conclusions and Inferences

2. Is it easy or hard to find **fossils**? Why?

_____

_____

3. What are some clues in the selection that lead you to believe that, long ago, the fossil layer was at the bottom of an ocean?

_____

_____

4. Why do The Rockfinders think **fossil** hunting is like being an explorer?

_____

_____

_____

_____

Part B

Read the selection below. Use the skills you have learned to answer the questions, choose the best answers, or complete the sentences.

Scarlett's Story

Two kittens huddled a few feet from a burning warehouse. Three other kittens were across the street. Their mother, a calico cat, gasped for breath. Her paws were scorched. Her blistered eyes were swollen.

Firefighter David Giannelli knew he saw an example of a mother's love. The four-week-old kittens were too young to have followed their mother out of the burning building. Their mother must have carried them out one-by-one. The cat and her kittens had **inhaled** smoke. When Giannelli placed them gently in a box, the mother cat touched each kitten with her injured nose and she hugged them with her scorched paws.

Soon, patches of red fur showed beneath the calico's **singed** fur. Workers in the shelter where the cat family had been taken named her Scarlett. Soon, people heard about Scarlett and calls came from Japan, South Africa, and the Netherlands. Everyone wanted to adopt Scarlett and her kittens. More than 7,000 letters arrived.

First, Scarlett had to heal. She was more severely injured than her kittens. Scarlett's kittens left the shelter first. Shelter workers **pampered** Scarlett for three months. It was her turn to be babied.

✓ Vocabulary

in•haled to draw in by breathing

singed to burn lightly

pam•per to treat with kindness

Facts and Details

1. How many kittens did Scarlett rescue?

Ⓐ 1   Ⓑ 2   Ⓒ 3   Ⓓ 5

Making Predictions

2. Which is the most likely outcome of Scarlett's story?

Ⓐ Scarlett went back to the burned building.

Ⓑ Scarlett took her kittens away.

Ⓒ After three months, the shelter workers found her a good home.

Ⓓ After three months, the shelter was closed down.

Conclusions and Inferences

3. According to the story, which is a conclusion that David Gianelli drew about Scarlett?

Ⓐ Her paws were scorched and her fur was singed.

Ⓑ More than 7,000 people wrote to the shelter.

Ⓒ Shelter workers **pampered** Scarlett for three months.

Ⓓ She must have carried her kittens out one by one.

Compare and Contrast

4. Write a sentence or two comparing what Scarlett did with what David Giannelli did.

_____

_____

_____

EXPLORING

Right now, as you read this sentence, scientists are getting ready to send human explorers to the red planet, Mars.

By the time you are a grown-up, the first trips will begin. Do you want to go? What will you find there? What will it look like? Where will you land? Will you find water? Will you find life?

In this unit you will read a story about the **exploration** of the planet Mars. You will get a chance to make predictions and figure out the meanings of new words from the context of the story. You will also learn about the amazing machines that scientists are sending to the planet so that people, maybe even you, can go there!

Vocabulary

ex•plo•ra•tion
the investigation or study of something

Think About It
What do you think the surface of Mars is like?
Ⓐ red and rocky   Ⓒ gray and dusty
Ⓑ green and grassy   Ⓓ blue and watery

Context Clues, Making Predictions **73**

AMAZING MACHINES IN OUTER SPACE

Vocabulary

re•mote con•trolled able to be controlled from far off or far away

probe a device used to explore or examine objects

Use words or picture clues in an article to figure out the meanings of unfamiliar words.

Imagine strange space crafts landing on a distant planet. One looks like a bunch of grapes and bounces on the surface. Others are **remote controlled** mini-cars, used to dig rocks from the ground with their robot arms.

Is this a story about an invasion of Earth? No! These are some of the amazing machines that scientists invented to send to Mars. Scientists are sending different kinds of space **probes** to gather information about the planet. This data will tell us many things: What is Mars like? What is it made of? Has there ever been life on it? Could we live on Mars?

React • Use Context Clues

What does the word **data** mean? What word clues from the article tell you the meaning of this word? Write a definition.

_____

_____

The exploration of Mars began in 1965 when the first **unmanned**, remote-controlled robotic spacecraft flew by the planet and sent back pictures. Ten years later, a robot lander touched down on Mars. The lander showed what the planet was like close up. Recently, scientists from around the world have planned **missions** for robots to explore Mars. These machines will send information back to Earth so we can learn all about the planet.

Some of the biggest questions that scientists have are about water. Is the water on Mars found today in the same place as water found in 1965? If not, where is it now?

We now know that Mars, like Earth, has frozen water at its north and south poles. Even though Mars seems to now be a desert, there are signs that water used to flow on its surface. Explorers may find water to drink in other places on the planet. It could also be a sign that Mars used to have plants or other living things of its own. It might still have them!

React • Make a Prediction

Write a sentence predicting what scientists may find when they land on the planet Mars.

_____

_____

When you make a prediction, you guess what might happen next.

sat•el•lite an object that travels around a planet, moon, or star

or•bit the path an object takes as it circles a planet

dune a rounded hill or ridge of sand

la•va hot, melted rock from a volcano

sam•ple a small amount of something

Scientists are learning more and more about Mars from these amazing machines. The Mars Global Surveyor **Satellite** began **orbiting** the planet in 1997. Each time it circled Mars, it helped scientists map the planet. Its close-up pictures showed new sand **dunes** from dust storms, and large pools of **lava** that flowed out of volcanoes millions of years ago.

Future probes will put tiny weather stations around Mars so its climate can be measured. Others may pick up and collect small bits of rock and return these **samples** to Earth. Robots can send information back from places too dangerous for people. This information will answer some of our questions about how to make Mars a place where humans can live one day soon.

Focus on Context Clues

★ **As you read, you will often discover unfamiliar words. The information that you get from the rest of a passage can help you understand the meaning of a new word.**

1. Look at familiar words around the highlighted word to figure out its meaning.

Its close-up pictures showed new sand **dunes** from dust storms, and large pools of lava that flowed out of volcanoes millions of years ago.

Dunes are

Ⓐ hills of sand.　Ⓑ ice caps.　Ⓒ craters.　Ⓓ meteors.

2. Reread "Amazing Machines in Outer Space."
Draw lines to match the new words to the clues.

Words	Clues

surveyor   flows out of volcanoes

satellite   circling a planet

orbiting   sand hills formed by wind

dunes   helps map the surface

lava   travels to a planet

3. What does **collect** mean? Read the sentence and
write a definition.

Others may pick up and **collect** small bits of
rock and return these samples to earth.

_____

_____

4. What does **lander** mean? Read the sentence and
write a definition.

Ten years later, a robot **lander** touched down on Mars.

_____

_____

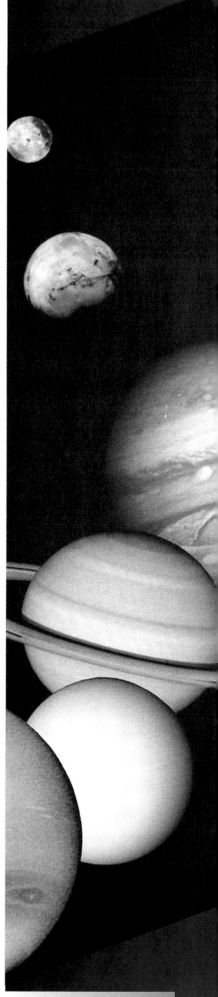

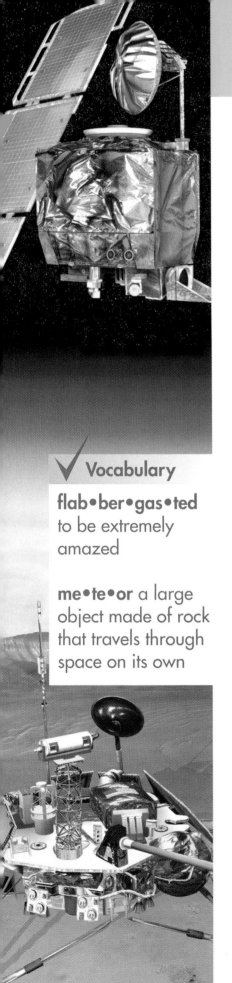

Focus on Making Predictions

Mars Mystery

Scientists stared at pictures that the Viking 1 Mars probe took in 1976. One image left some people **flabbergasted**. If it was what it seemed to be, it was the most amazing discovery ever made!

Photographs from one area of Mars appeared to show a huge stone carving of a human face. The photographs also seemed to show the remains of a city and a pyramid carved out of rock.

Scientists and geologists who study Mars for NASA disagreed. They said that the "face" and the "city" were natural rock formations made by the forces of wind, water, landslides, volcanoes, **meteor** craters, and lava on the surface of Mars.

At the moment, this seems to be the best explanation. Soon, robot cameras will give us all a closer look at Mars. The mystery may be solved.

★ **Predicting helps us use the information we read to understand what might happen in the future.**

Think about the discovery of mystery carvings on Mars. Complete each sentence by making a prediction about how different discoveries could change the way humans live on Mars.

1. If the probes find that there is underground water all over Mars, then. . .

_____

_____

✔ Vocabulary

flab•ber•gas•ted to be extremely amazed

me•te•or a large object made of rock that travels through space on its own

2. If the probes find that Mars has live volcanoes that pour out hot lava, then. . .

_____

_____

_____

_____

3. If it is true that the "face" on Mars was part of a Martian city, then. . .

_____

_____

_____

_____

4. If the probes find a populated city on Mars, then. . .

_____

_____

_____

_____

Destination Mars

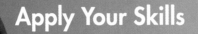

Scientists are working to **discover** ways that will allow humans to travel to Mars. The space station and space shuttle missions are ways scientists can study life in space. Once scientists know what life in space is like for short periods of time, then they can prepare for a long trip to Mars.

Other scientists are using robot **probes** to gather data about the surface of Mars so that they can plan human missions to land on Mars. At the same time, rocket engineers are working out better ways to make reusable rockets. Such **improvements** are making it less expensive to travel into space.

All this hard work is giving scientists new information and understanding that may help the US space agency NASA meet its goal to send humans to Mars by 2018.

Vocabulary

dis•cov•er to find or make known

probe a tool used to examine something

im•prove•ments ways that something is made better

1. Predict what might change if space travel was less expensive.

_____

_____

2. What clues can you find in the story that tell you what "engineers" build?

Ⓐ engines   Ⓑ stations   Ⓒ rockets   Ⓓ humans

3. Do you expect to hear more about Mars in the future? Why or why not?

_____

_____

4. What do the words **periods of time** mean? Read the sentence. Write a definition.

Once we know what life in space is like for short **periods of time**, then we can prepare for a long trip to Mars.

_____

_____

5. Complete the definition.

Making predictions helps us use the information we read to understand what might happen in the _____.

6. Write two reasons that will persuade your parents to send more robots into space. Make sure to predict two ways that robots will be valuable to people in the future.

_____

_____

_____

_____

_____

_____

Build Your Vocabulary

1. Read the conversation between Martin and Louie. Imagine how Louie answered using the words from the box.

probe	missions	dunes	data	orbit	samples

robotic   lava   meteor   flabbergasted   improvements

Martin: I can't believe it! My brother is going to explore Mars! What do you expect to see there?

Louie: _____

Martin: How do scientists know so much about Mars if no one has gone there before?

Louie: _____

Martin: Are you surprised that they picked you for the mission?

Louie: _____

2. Data is another word for

Ⓐ date.   Ⓑ information.   Ⓒ liquids.   Ⓓ fuel.

3. Craters are formed when _____ hit the surface of Mars.

Ⓐ scientists   Ⓑ meteors   Ⓒ volcanoes   Ⓓ lava

Did You Know?

The word **robot** comes from the Czech word *robata* which means "forced labor." It may have appeared first in a science fiction story by Karel Capek. In this story, machines looked like people. Write the name of a robot that you would make.

_____

Start with What You Know

Vocabulary

myth an old story usually explaining how something came to be

tra•di•tion the handing down of customs or beliefs

Tall Tales

Why do frogs swim? Why does the chipmunk have stripes? Native Americans created and told stories to answer these questions. As these stories were told over and over again, they became known as myths. A **myth** is a **traditional** story that has been told many times.

In animal myths, the animals can act like humans. They talk and have feelings. Native Americans believed animals and humans were related. They watched animals and learned from them.

Animal myths were told to show the children of a tribe how to act. Some myths were warnings. The adults hoped the stories would help children to be brave, kind, and wise.

In this unit you will read about the possum's tail, why frogs swim, and a myth about a chipmunk's stripes. Read each myth carefully. You will learn about recalling facts and details and sequence.

Think About It

Do you have a favorite animal story that has been read or told to you many times? Write a sentence about the story.

_____

_____

Sequence, Facts & Details **83**

Why Possum Has A Naked Tail

Here is a story from the Cherokee tribe of the southeast United States.

Long ago, Possum had a beautiful tail. It was long, bushy, and felt like silk. Possum was very proud of his tail. He loved to **brag** about it. "Isn't my tail wonderful?" Possum asked all the animals he met. "Feel how soft it is. Don't you wish your tail was this beautiful?"

At the animal **council** meetings he would boast about its beauty. "My tail is perfect. No one else has such a wonderful tail," he would say.

One day, Rabbit went to see Possum. "Possum, my friend," Rabbit said, "there is going to be a meeting. Our chief, Bear, wants you to sit beside him during the meeting. He will let you speak first because you have such a beautiful tail."

Possum was glad to hear Rabbit's news. "Bear is right. Isn't it the most perfect tail?" Rabbit looked at Possum's tail. "Your tail is very beautiful," Rabbit said. "But it looks dirty. I have a special medicine that will make it look the way it should."

Vocabulary

brag to boast about oneself or one's belongings

coun•cil a group of people who gather together to solve problems

React • Understand the Sequence

What did Rabbit tell Possum about his tail just before he put the medicine on it? Write a sentence to explain the sequence.

Rabbit mixed his medicine. It was very powerful. Possum's hairs began to fall out. But Rabbit wrapped an old snakeskin around Possum's tail. "The snakeskin will help the medicine work," Rabbit said. "Don't remove it until you are ready to speak at the meeting." Possum was excited. He wanted to take the skin off and see his beautiful tail, but he remembered Rabbit's words. All night he kept the snakeskin wrapped around his tail.

Possum was the first to arrive at the council meeting. A smile grew upon his face as he **imagined** the looks on the other animals' faces when they saw his tail. "Thanks to Rabbit's medicine, it will be more beautiful than ever," Possum thought. Finally the time was right. Possum began to peel off the snakeskin. "Look at my tail. Isn't it the finest tail you have ever seen?" As the snakeskin came off, so did all of the hair. Instead of a beautiful bushy tail, Possum's tail was naked and ugly.

Possum stared at his tail. His smile was still frozen on his face. He could not believe what had happened to his beautiful tail.

✓ **Vocabulary**

i•mag•ine to make up a picture or idea in your mind

Facts and details support the main idea of a paragraph.

React • Find Facts and Details

Find the facts and details about Possum's tail. The medicine made the hair on Possum's tail

Ⓐ soft and silky.

Ⓒ fall out.

Ⓑ long and bushy.

Ⓓ grow longer.

Possum was **ashamed** of his ugly tail. He wanted all the animals to stop looking at him. He wished he could run and hide. Instead, he fell to the ground and lay still as if he was dead. The grin stayed on his face until all the animals were gone.

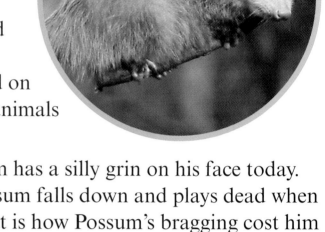

That is why Possum has a silly grin on his face today. That is also why Possum falls down and plays dead when he is scared. And that is how Possum's bragging cost him his beautiful tail. Today, he has the ugliest tail of all the animals.

Focus on Sequence

★ **When you read, it is important to understand the sequence or the order in which events happened. As you read, look for words such as *first*, *then*, *next*, *before*, and *after* to help you.**

1. Reread the story. Number the following sentences in the order they happened in the story.

_____ Rabbit put medicine on Possum's tail.

_____ Rabbit wrapped a snakeskin around Possum's tail.

_____ The powerful medicine caused Possum's hair to fall out.

_____ Rabbit told Possum his tail was dirty.

2. Read the passage on page 86. Write a sentence to tell what Possum did after the snakeskin came off.

_____

_____

3. In the boxes below, draw a picture of what Possum's tail looked like before and after Rabbit put medicine on it.

"Before"	"After"

4. Sequence the events in the story by completing the chart.

First	
Next	
After That	
Then	
Finally	

Focus on Facts and Details

As you read the myths, pay attention to the details and ask yourself these questions:

★ **What do the characters look like?**

★ **How do the characters act?**

★ **Where does the story take place?**

1. Think back to the story of the possum. Draw a line to match the questions to their answers in the chart below.

What did Possum like to show off?	snakeskin
What did Possum's tail look like in the past?	medicine
Who was the chief of the animals?	silky tail
What made Possum's hair fall out?	next to bear
What did Rabbit wrap around Possum's tail?	hairless
Where did Possum sit at the council meeting?	beautiful
What does Possum's tail look like now?	bear

Why Frogs Swim

Long ago, frogs lived only on the land, not the water.

One day, Mother Frog was watching her baby play near the **riverbank**. Along came a snake. As Snake got closer, he hissed in disgust. "Hsss! Yuck! Your baby smells awful! Don't you ever bathe her?"

"No," Mother Frog replied.

"That is why she stinks," said Snake. He **slithered** away.

Mother Frog thought about it. She picked up her child and tossed her in the river. SPLASH!

Some time later, Snake returned. "Where is your smelly baby?" he asked.

"I tossed her in the river," she answered.

"But I only told you to bathe her," Snake said.

"Well, she's in the river now, that's were she'll stay."

Today, frogs live in the water and know how to swim. And since they do not stink, snakes eat them whenever they can.

Vocabulary

riv•er•bank the ground along the edge of a river

slith•er to move along the ground by sliding

2. What did Snake notice about the baby frog?

Ⓐ She was a baby.

Ⓑ She was a frog.

Ⓒ She was green.

Ⓓ She was smelly.

3. Baby frog had never

Ⓐ played in the mud.

Ⓑ hopped in the grass.

Ⓒ taken a bath.

Ⓓ jumped near the riverbank.

How Chipmunk Got His Stripes

Long ago, Bear liked to brag, "No animal is greater than I am. There is nothing I can not do."

"I know something you can not do," a soft voice said. Bear looked down and saw a Chipmunk. Chipmunk challenged Bear to stop the sun from rising in the morning. Bear accepted, and the two spent the night facing east.

Vocabulary

mut•ter to speak quietly with lips almost closed

whis•per to speak in a low soft voice

All night Bear **muttered**, "The sun will not rise." Chipmunk **whispered**, "The sun WILL rise.

After many hours, a faint light appeared. Bear yelled, "Do not rise!" But the sun continued to rise. "Ha!" teased Chipmunk. "You could not stop the sun from rising."

Angry, Bear chased Chipmunk across the forest and into his hole. Bear's claw scratched three stripes across Chipmunk's back. Chipmunk still has those stripes today.

1. What happened before Chipmunk slid into his hole? What happened after Chipmunk slid into his hole? Write a sentence to tell about before and after.

_____

_____

2. Which direction did Bear and Chipmunk face all night?

Ⓐ North   Ⓒ West

Ⓑ South   Ⓓ East

3. Why did Bear and Chipmunk sit up all night?
Write a sentence using facts and details from the story.

_____

_____

4. What does the story tell you about the kind of animals
they were? Use details from the story.

Chipmunk is_____

Bear is_____

5. How would Chipmunk describe Bear?

_____

_____

_____

6. Write a list telling the sequence of the chipmunk story.
Use numbers and full sentences.

_____

_____

_____

_____

Build Your Vocabulary

Complete each sentence by writing a word from the box.

brag	council	riverbank	after	slither	mutter
	east	chipmunk	ashamed	before	

1. The chipmunk got his stripes _____ he slid down the hole.

2. Possum would _____ about his tail to all the other animals. Use this word in another sentence about Bear.

   _____

   _____

3. After his hair fell out, Possum was _____ of his hairless tail.

4. Name another animal that is described as hairless or featherless on some part of its body. Hint: this animal flies and is a famous American symbol.

   _____

5. Which animal from the myths was your favorite? Write a sentence about your favorite animal using words from the box.

   _____

Did You Know

Riverbank is a compound word made up of two smaller words: **river** and **bank**. Can you think of any other compound words?

_____

Part A

Read the selection below. Use the skills you have learned to answer the questions, choose the best answers, or complete the sentences.

How the Supermarket Checkout Works

Have you noticed the **bar codes** on products in supermarkets? Bar codes are made up of black bars and white spaces. Here is an example of a bar code.

Bar codes tell the supermarket checkout computer what each item in your grocery cart costs. When you make a purchase, the supermarket assistant moves the item over a window that lies flat next to the cash register. An invisible infrared **laser** beams onto the bar code. Then the computer in the cash register reads the information and shows the price of what you bought on a screen.

✓ Vocabulary

bar code black bars and white spaces on a product that tell what the product costs

la•ser a very narrow and strong beam of light

Summarizing

1. Which statement best summarizes the selection?

Ⓐ Bar codes tell if you should pay cash.

Ⓑ Bar codes tell the computer in the cash register how much to charge.

Ⓒ Bar codes are black and white.

Ⓓ Bar codes work with laser beams.

Context Clues

2. The word **infrared** in paragraph 2 probably has something to do with

 Ⓐ windows.   © checking out.

 Ⓑ light.   Ⓓ paying cash.

3. A good synonym for the word **assistant** in paragraph 2 is

 Ⓐ secretary.   © worker.

 Ⓑ sergeant.   Ⓓ checker.

Sequence

4. What happens when the assistant moves the bar code over the window?

_____

_____

5. What happens before you reach the supermarket checkout?

_____

_____

6. What happens after the infrared laser beams onto the bar code?

_____

_____

Part B

Read the selection below. Use the skills you have learned to answer the questions, choose the best answers, or complete the sentences.

Gymnast's Spirit Survives Tough Break

Vocabulary

sev•ered kept or put apart, separated

fused blended together thoroughly, joined

It was December 31, 1998. A seventeen-year-old girl with a shy smile greeted Mayor Rudolph Giuliani and the city of New York. Thousands cheered the girl. She waved back from her wheelchair.

People had been cheering this young girl's spirit for months. Sang Lan, a Chinese gymnast, had traveled to the United States in July 1998. A head-first fall during a practice vault cut short her hopes to win at the Goodwill Games. The fall broke Sang Lan's neck and **severed** her spinal cord.

Doctors worked to help her. First, they **fused** the broken bones in her neck. An experimental drug was given to heal her spinal cord. Still, she was told, she may not walk again.

Some might have despaired. But, many years before, Sang Lan had learned to work hard to overcome setbacks, and to smile while doing it. She kept smiling while she overcame this first setback. She set high goals after her injury. She wants to walk again. The whole world wants that for her, too. Keep smiling, Sang Lan!

Sequence

1. What happened as Sang Lan took a practice vault?

_____

_____

2. What was the first thing doctors did to repair Sang Lan's broken neck?

_____

_____

3. Number the following events from Sang Lan's life in the order in which they occurred.

_____ Sang Lan had learned to work hard to overcome setbacks, and to smile while doing it.

_____ She set high goals after her injury.

_____ Doctors worked to help her.

_____ Sang Lan, a Chinese gymnast, had traveled to the United States in July, 1998.

_____ The fall broke Sang Lan's neck and severed her spinal cord.

Fact and Opinion

4. Write F for fact or O for opinion next to each statement.

_____ If Sang Lan had not broken her neck, she would have won her event in the Goodwill Games.

_____ Sang Lan wants to walk again.

_____ The experimental drug will heal her spinal cord.